I0061544

A Critical Analysis of Vijay Tendulkar's Kamala

Dr. Beena A. Mahida

CANADIAN
Academic Publishing

2014

Copyright © 2014. Beena Mahida

All rights reserved. This book or any portion thereof may not be reproduced or used in any manner whatsoever without the express written permission of the publisher except for the use of brief quotations in a book review or scholarly journal.

Price : $27.86

First Edition : December, 2014

ISBN :   978-1-926488-18-9

ISBN Allotment Agency : Library and Archives Canada (Govt. of Canada)

Published & Printed by
Canadian Academic Publishing
81, Woodlot Crescent,
Etobicoke,
Toronto, Ontario, Canada.
Postal Code- M9W 6T3
Phone- +1 (647) 633 9712
http://www.canadapublish.com

PREFACE

Art is inevitable part of human culture. Art is knowledge coupled with emotions. Human interest in art has been eternal and this eternity has made man civilized and cultured. Art is concerned with expression and man expresses himself through any form of art. Drama has always remained a unique means to spread morality and to entertain. Drama in India has a long history and in regional languages it is as popular as other literary genres – fiction and poetry. In Indian Literature, drama in English has not attained much popularity because plays in regional languages dominate the theatre. In recent times, Plays in the regional languages are translated in to English and such translations have established link between East and West, and North and South as well as harmony and unity in modern India.

In this context Vijay Tendulkar's Marathi Plays occupy a unique place. When I read the English translation of Tendulkar's plays I decided to pursue my research on plays of Tendulkar and in this decision Dr.R.K.Madalia of the Department of English provided much needed help by accepting to become my Supervisor for the research. He suggested to carry out my research on Tendulkar's major 6 (six) plays and to analyse them from the point of view of characterization, themes and dramatic techniques. Each of the plays of Tendulkar presented new perspective which made stimulating reading.

Tendulkar has not contributed to the modern Marathi theatre but has given it a new dimension. His plays disturb the audience by raising complex issues that remain unsettled even today in modern India. Tendulkar is not feminist but women are at the center in his plays. He treats his women characters with understanding and compassion against men who are selfish and hypocritical.

I have tried my level best in analyzing the different aspects of Tendulkar's Plays yet I believe that literature offers vast spectrum and if something is left out in my research, I leave it to future scholars to pursue studies that are more elaborate. This book is slight modification of the thesis. I have separated each play for a separate book to get wider information regarding the play and the details within and tried to focus in details the themes, characters, and important aspects.

Ghashiram Kotwal is set in eighteenth century Pune at the time of the Peshwa rule. The play features the Peshwa's chancellor Nana Phadnavs and when it was first staged it came up against a lot of criticism of or showing the revered Nana's character in a derogatory light. In my view Ghashiram Kotwal indicates a particular social situation which is neither old nor new. It is beyond time and space. Therefore 'Ghashiram' and Nana Phadnavis are are also beyond space and time'.

The success or failure of any work of art depends upon its appeal – whether that appeal proves to be transitory or everlasting. A work of art with an everlasting appeal always remains eternal. It will not be out of the way or excessive exaggeration if the same thing is said about Tendulkar's plays.

Dr. Beena A. Mahida

CONTENTS

Preface

1.	Introduction	1 – 30
2.	Kamala : An Overview	31 – 36
3.	Progress Oriented Modern Man	37 – 43
4.	Condition of Women in Independent India	44 – 60
5.	Investigative Journalism v/s Gandhian Journalism	61 – 66
7.	Dramatic Techniques in Kamala	67 – 73
8.	Conclusion	74 – 80

Bibliography

1. INTRODUCTION

Drama has always remained a unique means to spread morality and to entertain. Long before movies came into being Indian theatre had been a major source of spreading moral value and entertainment. The remarkable feature is that- in spite of the emergence of the Indian cinema, the Indian theatre has not lost significance.

The Indian cinema with all its advanced techniques, sophisticated cameras and freedom of variety has remained unsuccessful in surpassing the Indian Theatre. No doubt – an actor who works in a cinema gets more money than a player of the stage but- the player of the stage gets more appreciation than the actor on the screen. The camera of a movie allows the compensation of a re-take to the actor whereas for the artist of a theatre no re-take is possible. His work demands more sincerity and higher efficiency which finally bring greater appreciation to him.

The tradition of Indian Drama is very old. It goes back to the Sanskrit Drama of ancient India. India being a large country with diverse cultures and regional languages has various traditions of form and matter, distinct and yet having many common factors of dramaturgy. Modern Indian drama is influenced not only by classical Sanskrit drama or local folk forms but also by western theatre following the establishment of British rule in India.

N. S. Dharan, an eminent writer of Indian writing in English writes "Drama in India has a long history". Girish Karnad says that the earliest extant play in India was written as early as A.D. 200. Dating to the days of Bhasa, Bhavabuti and Kalidasa, drama can boast of a rich and chequered history. The early plays were written in Sanskrit, based on the Vedas and the Upanishads. In fact, the Vedas and the Upanishads have never ceased to be sources of inspiration to man of letters both in India and abroad. Down the centuries, Indian drama has undergone various metamorphoses and it still continues to flourish in all regional languages. In regional languages it enjoys almost an equal status along with two other major literary genres, namely fiction and poetry. In Indian literature drama in English is yet to register an appreciable growth. By and large, plays written in regional languages dominate the Indian theatre. These plays are easily intelligible to the audiences. Actors too can easily improvise in them.

Several regional amateur theatres have also flourished from time to time. In the post-Independence period, performing arts were employed as an effective means of public enlightenment during the First-Five year plan (1951-54). As a result the National school of Drama was established under the directorship Alkhazi. Institutions for training in dramatics were founded in big cities. Drama departments started functioning in several universities. The annual Drama Festival was started in New Delhi by the Sangit Natak Akademi in 1954. With so much encouragement coming from so many quarters, drama began to flourish in the regional languages.

During the last few years, several plays, originally written in the regional languages, have been translated into English. Today, a sizeable number of such plays do exist. According to many academicians, it is necessary to incorporate these translations into the corpus of Indian English Literature as they also contribute an important component to it. Such translations of plays have forged an effective link between the East and the West the North and the South of India and contributed, in no small measure, to the growing harmony and richness of contemporary creative consciousness.

According to **Indranath Chaudhary**, when the sahitya Akademi was set up in 1954, Dr. S. Radhakrishnan spelt out its objective as the promotion of the unity of Indian literature, despite India's geographical, political, Social, and Linguistic diversities. Dr. Radhakrishnan gave a slogan to the Akademi that Indian literature is one, though written in many languages. It is in this context that the plays of Girish Karnad in Kannada, Mohan Rakesh in Hindi, Badal Sircar in Bengali and Vijay Tendulkar in Marathi occupy a unique place as pointed out by **Arundhati Banerjee** :

"In the 1960s four dramatisls from different regions of India writing in their own regional languages were said to have ushered modernity in to the sphere of Indian drama and theatre. They were Mohan Rakesh in Hindi, Badal Sircar in Bengali and Vijay Tendulkar in Marathi and Girish Karnad in Kannada. Rakesh's untimely death left his life's work incomplete, and Karnad has written only intermittently. Sircar, of course, has been almost as active as Tendulkar though his plays can be divided in to three distinct periods. Tendulkar, however, has not only been the most productive but has also introduced the greatest variations in his dramatic creations."

V. B. Deshpande rightly states, "Since the Independence – since 1950, to be precise – the name of Vijay Tendulkar has been in the forefront of the Marathi drama and stage. His personality both as man and writer is multifaceted. It has often been puzzling and curious with a big question mark on it. In the last 55 years he has written stories, novels, one – act plays, plays for children as well adults. Similarly he has done script6 writing and news paper columns as well. And in all these fields he has created an image of his own. Thus he is a creative writer with a fine sensibility and at the same time a contemplative and controversial dramatist. He has made a mark in the field of journalism also. Because of his highly individual viewpoint and vision of life and because of his personal style of writing he has made a powerful impression in the field of literature and drama, and has given the post-independence, Marathi drama a new idiom. By doing this he has put Marathi drama on the national and international Map."

The same indebtedness is expressed by **Arundhati Banerjee** "Vijay Tendulkar has been in the vanguard of not just Marathi but Indian theatre for almost forty years".He not only pioneered the experimental theatre movement in Marathi but also guided it."

While talking about contemporary Marathi Theatre **Dhyaneshwar Nadkarni** points out,

"Vijay Tendulkar leads the vanguard of the avant garde theatre that developed as a movement separate from the mainstream. Tendulkar and his colleagues were dissatisfied with the decadent professional theatre that characterized the Thirties and Forties. They wanted to give theatre a new form and therefore experimented with all aspects of it including content, acting décor and audience communication."

Chandrasekhar Barve expresses a similar opinion about Tendulkar's contribution to Marathi theatre,

"We can say with certainty that Tendulkar has guided Marathi drama that seemed to have lost its proper track, and has kept leading it for over two decades. His place and importance in this respect shall remain unique in the history of Marathi drama.

There may be controversies regarding his greatness but his achievements are beyond question.

He has written 28 full length plays, 24 one-act plays, several middles, articles, editorials and 11 plays for children. In spite of his success in every genre, his versatility as a writer has been overshadowed by his fame as a dramatist since drama has been his forte.

Mr. Barve observes,

"His extra-dramatic writing also reveals his pure taste for drama which tries to capture the different tensions and through them, finds "dramatics" accurately".His one-act plays are more experimental than his full-length plays. Most of them have been translated and produced in major Indian languages and some of them into English.

Vijay Tendulkar was born in **1928** at **Bombay** in **Maharastra**. He was born and brought up in Kandevali, a small lane in Girgaon. A lower middle class community dwelt. There and the males were mostly the shopkeepers and clerks. He was living in a typical chawl, in apartments of one room, kitchen, balcony and common toilets, so Tendulkar's upbringing in a lower middle class community provided him chance to perceive middle class minutely which helped him to portray its different shades on the stage.

His **father Mr. Dhondopant Tendulkar** was a head clerk at a British publishing firm called Longmans Green and company (Now Orient Longman). His **mother Mrs. Susheela Tendulkar** was a housewife. His father was a writer, director and actor of amateur Marathi plays. He didnot join the commercial drama company as formerly a career in the theatre was not honoured. Four years old Tendulkar used to go with his father to the rehearsals so he nurtured love for the theatre from his childhood. Tendulkar himself considers those rehearsals as a kind of "Magic show". Because like magic he saw the living beings change into characters. He saw with wonder the male performing the roles of woman by changing their voice and movements. He didn't have any exposure to other theatre except what his father staged.

Tendulkar had other **brother** named **Raghunath** and **sister Leela**. His two elder sisters died in infancy. He had two younger brothers but- he was the favourite child of his parents. He was sickly child and suffering from cough and asthmatic wheezing. So special care, protection and love were provided to this sickly boy by the parents for fear of losing him if not protected well. He was given the **pet name "Papia"** and above all he was known as a **"Mother's child"** being favourite of his mother. Emotionally he was more attached with his mother than his father. He remembers how his mother used to feed him forcefully.

Due to his unhealthy body the family servant used to take him to school. It was municipal school. As usual it had small dingy rooms with awful toilets and it had no playground and water at times. In the school also special attention was given to him as he belonged to somewhat well to do family. His teachers used to borrow story books from him and by becoming partial they left him alone at the examination. Thus he studied in an average Indian school, which has no basic facilities but he carries those moments in comparison with sophisticated school where he studied later in life. At 9 years of age he attended "Chikisaha samooha", where he found himself totally strange among the sophisticated children and spacious buildings.

Tendulkar surprisingly started his career as a **writer** at a very early stage of life. He wrote stories and essays when he was **6** years of age. His father was a writer, director and actor so creativity was inborn in him. The unpublished work of his father lay at home and little Tendulkar passed his time with books and had read novel and short stories of eminent writers so he grew up in a literary atmosphere. The seed had already been sown in little mind for literature and gradually it took the shape of huge tree.

He had never imagined himself to be a writer in his childhood. As a small child he wanted to be an engine driver or an acrobat in circus and dreamt of wondering from place to place astonishing the crowd by daredevil acts. He used to visit fairs and circus with his father which were like big fairyland for him. So childlike curiosity, interest and amazement surrounded him along with his keen interest in reading. Sunday and vacation had special attraction for him. On Sunday morning his father used to take him to a large bookshop of his friend used to buy books of his choice. In evening his father took him to chowpatty beach and they travelled in train from Charni Road to Colaba which attracted him a lot. During summer vacation the family used to go for Goa or to Port Ratnagiri.

Tendulkar remembers that his father was a strict disciplinarian, impractical, stubborn but an honest man. "To be honest is a disqualification in todays world" and so Mr. Dhondopant Tendulkar never got the honour of being honest and idealist. He never took bribes or extra fees. But he felt proud to be poor and was very much content with life. Due to this the later life of his father was miserable. The elder brother Raghunath quarrelled with him and left the home. His father was against the dowry system and so Tendulkar's sister Leela didn't get married and had to remain single. It seems that the father had never got family love due to certain principles.

Apart from the influence of the father, Raghunath, his brother also played formative influence on Tendulkar. His brother was a follower of Gandhi and Gandhian principles. He used to attend political congress meetings. The father wanted him to be active in studies but he went astray. He wanted to marry Hansa Wadkar which was unbearable for the idealist father and so the family separated from Raghunath and moved to Kolhapur. Tendulkar used to get gifts like pastries, sweets and pen from his brother. He used to go for English movies with his brother. But his brother died miserably due to alchoholic habit.

The later childhood of Tendulkar passed at Kolhapur – a princely state in Maharastra. At Kolhapur he made himself noticeable by his excellence in reciting English poems. When he was **11 years** old, he **wrote** and **directed** and **acted "Maya Bazaar".** This way, the journey of this veteran writer towards performing arts started. At Kolhapur his friend was the son of one prominent playwright named Na vi kulkarni, who shared the same literary interest with Tendulkar. He even worked as a **child artist** in **two Marathi** Films.

As a teenager, at the **age** of **13** the family shifted to Pune and he attended a new school. He believed that he might have completed matriculation but the **Quit India Movement** was in momentum and Tendulkar was one of those who obeyed Gandhi's call to boycott the school. He started taking part in campaign against Britishers and he used to attend the early morning meetings without informing his parents. At the **age** of **14** while attending such meeting, he **was arrested** and the family came to know about Tendulkar's active participation in freedom fighting. Again he attended the school but now he started bunking the classes and developed the habit of spending the monthly fees of the **school** in watching English films. The visuals had a good impact on him. This exposure to the theatre at an early age has had its strong influence on him as a **successful** dramatist. He says in an interview, "As a school boy I had watched the Hollywood films playing in my hometown, not once, but each one over and over again. I still remember the visuals, not the dialogues which I didn't understand. A more conscious education in what the visual could do came when I worked with the Rangayan Theatre group in Bombay, but watching Marcel Marceau from the last seat in the last row was an enthralling experience. Not a single word was uttered, but so much was expressed. After that I wrote mimes for quite a while. I felt the visual had unlimited possibilities, the word was useless. But I am a playwright, words are my tools, I had to use them." Apart from Films he denoted his time at the city library in reading which helped him a lot during his career as a journalist. But his father was disappointed seeing the poor prospect of Tendulkar.

At Pune, Tendulkar found the **Role Model** of his life – **Dinkar BalKrishna Mokashi,** a radio mechanic but a good writer. He led a very simple life and Tendulkar was impressed by his personality and the informality of his writing style. His other **Role Model** was **Vishnu Vinayak Bokil,** a teacher and a writer. Tendulkar liked his light hearted, jovial and exuberant style. He remembered one incident of the school when Mr. Vinayak asked the students to look at the names of rank holders of the school on the board and asked, "Where are those top rankers now? Does anyone know?"Then he said that the students should pass the exam as the parents pay the fees but the marks they get were not everything. He advised them to develop their personality in other directions also. It worked as a boosting to the teen Tendulkar to look beyond the school. Later on, as a writer Tendulkar dedicated one of his book to this school teacher Mr. Vinayak.

At 16, Tendulkar **left the school** for good. He had no friends and no any communication with his parents. He wanted to talk! But with whom! He had to talk with himself! And he put all his dialogues with his own self on paper through various forms-poems stories, film scripts and at this stage of his life his writing acquired a conscious motivation.

At the age of **22** he wrote his **First full length original play "Grihastha"** which flopped like anything and he took an oath that he would never write a play in life and to his surprise he has written **28 full length** plays as well as he has been **working actively** in the theatre world for the last **45 years.**

He always considers himself a writer first and a playwright after words. About his love for writing he writes,

"The point is more than a playwright, I consider myself to be a writermeaning I loved to indulge in the physical process of writing. I enjoy this process even when there is nothing to be said. Give me a piece of paper any paper and pen and I shall write as naturally as a bird flies or a fish swims. Left to myself, I scribble. And I never get tired of writing... Especially when I write in my mother tongue i.e. Marathi. Writing gives me a pleasure which has no substitute. However, tired I am physically or mentally, the moment I pick up the pen and begin running it on a paperany piece of paper I feel good I feel refreshed I feel as if I am born again. Writing by itself is a luxury for me. When I write, I forget myself, I forget my anxieties..."

He has been writing in different roles by using different mediums. He was **journalist**. He had been **sub-editor** and executive editor in journals and assistant editor of a daily. He used to write editorials with the information received from the second hand sources. This filled him with great dissatisfaction. He says,

"It started with my journalistic dissatisfaction but it grew into much bigger proportions in the sense that it became a matter of conscience as a human being. I became restless."

The violence, the oppression and the exploitation in the society that he witnessed made him restless. And journalism could not offer him a viable solution for his mental agitation. But it does shape his dramatic career. **Gowri Ramnarayan**, therefore points out: "With his exposure to Marathi theatre from childhood, and journalistic background Vijay Tendulkar turned contemporary socio-political situations into explosive drama."

His desire was to start a daily newspaper column and he enjoyed **writing a column** for **six months** in 1993, when Babri Masjid was destroyed. And during those six months he didn't write anything but only enjoyed column writing. He well remembered that during his journalistic days he sometimes wrote for astrology column, when the 'official' astrologer did not reach in time and he enjoyed in forecasting bright future for the unknown readers of the column. As a writer he found good fun in playing the **role** of **an astrologer**.

Being versatile he can put himself in any role. During the period of struggle he did **Ghost writing** with full knowledge that his name would not appear and become known to the readers. He took it as a role with its own "character". His inner personality as a writer underwent a natural change to suit the role. Along with his job in a newspaper he started writing short story and play and even Ghost writing for additional income. His writing developed according to the demands of the roles. He also worked as a **Public Relation Officer** in an industry and wrote copy for add-agencies. He **translated** American Books for the united information services and wrote **scripts** for non-descript Government Documentaries. He played different roles in order to earn his livelihood but his writing practice has brought perfection in writing skill.

Vijay Tendulkar, as a sensitive, sensible and responsible citizen, could not quieten his agitated conscience with his journalistic career. So he left journalism when he received Nehru Fellowship for the 1973-75. During this period, he travelled extensively throughout India and saw directly all kinds of violence. **From this experience, he infers:**

"Unlike communists I don't think that violence can be eliminated in a classless society, or, for that matter, in any society. The spirit of aggression is something that the human being is born with. Not that it's bad. Without violence man would have turned into a vegetable."So he perceived both the positive and negative faces of violence.

Regarding ideology he says,

"I do not align myself to any political ideology.......I do have my sympathies with the left"He does not subscribe to any ideology in his plays. Nor does he write for commercial purpose.

Moreover, in the words of **Mr. Barve,**

"Tendulkar's plays helped to refine Marathi drama that was so far polluted by propaganda for political awakening and social reforms, cheap and vulgar entertainment". Tendulkar does not subscribe to any particular political Ideologies, as they, including Marxism, are unable to understand the complex human situation and to suggest any viable solution to our Hydra-headed problems. Yet he does not lack political awareness.

He says to **Gowri Ramnarayan** in an interview,

"I had a political background, I was involved in the 1942 movement.Journalism developed my political sense, curiosity for instance ....naturally this got in my writing."

He was actively associated with civil liberties movements in Maharashtra. All this shows his great concern for his country and society. He is a realist and refuses to be fooled by romantic concepts of reforms and movements. He exposed the flaws and the inevitable failure of unrealistic reforms and movements in his plays.

Mr. Tendulkar considers himself as an **actor-writer** and himself acted on the stage during his apprentice days in the theatre but did not find it as exciting as writing. He was an actor on the stage of his creative mind. According to him he acts as he writes in his mind he emotes the **lives** of the character as he writes. They are not written words but a total and spontaneous expression of the mind and the personality of the character which includes not only the words but also the eloquent silence in between the words-broken sentences, the subtle emphasis on certain words, even the pitch of the voice, the gestures of the hands. He can 20 visualize the position of the characters on the stage – the total composition of the scene and even the lighting. Thus he acted their speech, behavior patterns and their ways of looking at things. So he believes he can act better than others because he has acted his play out when he wrote the play. **Mr. Tendulkar** was basically **a man of theatre**, which he had inherited from his father and eldest brother. He had a curiosity for this performing art and subconscious and unquenched desire to explore the magic and beauty of this form. His love for the theatre continued as he wrote plays at school, acted in plays, watched it, discussed it and for the last 45 years he was in the world of theatre. He believes that performing art is addictive.

He writes,

"You can learn the "grammar" but art is not mere grammar. It is an expression it provides endless learning by experiments, by committing mistakes."

He remembered that at a very early stage of his life he had developed curiosity for people and consciously noted the speech habits of people, their manners and personal peculiarities. He gives an expression to it in his writing so some of his characters are related to certain living persons. He believed that the creative process is complicated process. The characters would appear in utter chaos till he conceives it. He could never write a play with only idea or theme in mind but he needed character first with him. He writes,

"I could not proceed to write a play unless I saw my characters as real life people, unless I could see them moving doing things by themselves, unless I heard them emoting, talking to each other, I was never able to begin writing my play only with an idea or a theme in mind. I had to have my characters first with me ...." Thus, they are not puppets but living persons of distinction.

About the structuring of his play he said he had never attended any courses for this skill but he had learnt it by trial and error method which is very costly. He wrote that one has to own money in experimental theatre. No one sponsors the play and by the time the players correct the mistakes they are doing the last show of the play. For him, the Rehearsal Hall had become the learning ground. In absence of theatrical devices the inner mechanism of a play with its positive and negative points were laid open and he learnt a lot from these brain- storming rehearsal sessions. Apart from experimenting in the theatre, watching rehearsals he used to see play every day once, twice or thrice in one day. He did not bother whether the play is good or bad but it helped him in internalizing the techniques of playwriting – especially the structuring of the play.

He learnt a lot by watching films because a film also has to have a structure. Even the **concerts** of **classical music impressed** him though he did not know its grammar but classical music has its strict rules and regulations. The **reading** of **the poems** also supplied him the knowledge about compact structure and a form. The visit to the **Art Galleries** made him aware about the rhythm, form and structure in good painting. Apart from all these **Peter Brook's** Book (Master Craftsman in the art of Theatre) taught him the foremost principles of theatre world that all visual art including the art of the theatre, have one thing in common- The space, and it is the skill of the dramatist that how meaningfully and ingeniously he fills the space.

Arundhati Banerjee says,

"Tendulkar's first major work that set him apart from previous generation Marathi playwrights was *Manus Navache Bel (An Island called Man)* (1955). His dramatic genius was cutout for the newly emerging, experimental Marathi theatre of the time. His direct association with Rangayan at this point of his career and continous interaction with such theatre personalities as Vijaya Mehta, Arvind and Sulabha Despande, Kamalakar Sarang Madhav Vatve and Damoo Kenkre provided new impetus for creative faculties. Thus Manus Navache Bel was closely followed by a spate of plays (1958). *Madhlya Bhinti (The walls Between) Chimnicha Ghar Hota Menacha (Nest of wax) (1958) Mee Jinklo Mee Harlo (I won, I lost) (1963) Kavlanchi Shala (school for crows) (1963) and Sari Ga Sari (Rain o Rain) (1964)* which would chart the course of avant-grade Marathi theatre during the next few years. There seems to be a consistency of theme and treatment in them despite the apparently desperate nature of their subjects. In all these early plays, Tendulkar is concerned with the middle class individual set against the backdrop of a hostile society."

Most of Tendulkar's plays are in the naturalistic writing. However, his Ghashiram Kotwal is in the folk tradition while his last two plays *Niyatioya Bailala (To Hell with Destiny)* and *Safar (The Tour)* emplay fantasy. The play **"Silence! The court is in session"** (1967) made him the centre of a general controversy. He has already been called the angry young man of the Marathi theatre. He was considered a rebel against the established values of a fundamentally orthodox society **Encounter in** Umbugland (1974) is a political allegory (1971) **The Vultures** shocked the conservative sections of Marathi people with its naturalistic display of cupidity, sex, and violence. **Sakharam Binder** (1972) is probably Tendulkar's most intensely naturalistic play and shocked the conservative society even more than **The Vultures**. In **Ghashiram Kotwal** (1972) he moves from the naturalistic writing in to the folk tradition, it explains the power game that are found in Indian politics. **Kamala** (1981) is based on **a** real life incident reported in The Indian Express by Ashwin sarin. Kanyadaan is also one of the controversial play and branded as anti – Dalit play. It actually tries to show how our romantic idealism fails.

He wrote his plays in Marathi, First, he influenced Marathi theatre and guided it. Later, his impact extended to other Indian languages as his plays were translated into them. Tendulkar perceived the realities of the human society without any reconceived notions, reacted to them as a sensitive and sensible human being and wrote about them in his plays as a responsible writer. He never wrote to win a prize or an award.

He says,

"I have written about my own experience and about what I have seen in others around me. I have been true to all this and have not cheated my generation. I did not attempt to simplify matters and issues for the audience when presenting my plays, though that would have been easier occupation. Sometimes my plays jolted society out of its stupor and I was punished. I faced this without regrets. It is an old habit with me to do what I am told not to do. My plays could not have been anything else. They contain my perceptions of society and its value and I cannot write what I do not perceive".

In his plays he deals with the issues of gender inequality, social inequality, power games, self alienation, sex and violence. His characters are very much real. They are neither completely good nor completely bad. He liberated Marathi stage from the tyranny of conventional theatre with its mild doses of social and political satire for purpose of pure entertainment.

Mr. M. Sarat Babu writes,

"Vijay Tendulkar portrays the contemporary society and the predicament of man in it with a special focus on the morbidity in his plays, which remind us of Nietzche's words "the disease called man" and also Freud's description of human civilization as "a universal neurosis". His plays touch almost every aspect of human life in the modern world and share the disillusionment of the post modern intellectuals, however they seem to highlight three major issues : gender, power and violence."

Vijay Tendulkar devoted his life for the world of theatre as he says ,

"What I like about those years is that they made me grow as a human being. And theatre which was my major concern has contributed to this in a big way. It helped me to analyse my own life and the lives of others. It led me to make newer and newer discoveries in the vast realm of the human mind which still defies all available theories and logic. It is like an everintriguing puzzle or a jungle which you can always enter but has no way out..."Such a prolific and versatile writer has been felicitated with many awards and honours like

1. The Maharashtra State Government Award (1956, 1969 and 1973)

2. The Sangeet Natak Akademi Award (1971)

3. The Filmfare Award (script writer) (1980,1983)

4. The Padmabhushan (1984)

5. The Saraswati Samman (1993)

6. The Kalidas Samman (1999)

7. The Maharashtra Gaurav Puraskar (1999)

8. The Jansthan Award (1999)

9. Katha Chudamani Award (2001)

This legendary theatre man passed away on **19th May, 2008**. He was suffering from Myasthenia Gravis, a neuromuscular disease. He died at the age of 80 in a private hospital at Pune where he was hospitalized since 10th April, 2008. Shirish Prayag, Director of Prayag Hospital stated, "At the time of his demise he was extremely calm and quiet. There was an expression of contentment on his face. His face did not reflect any pain."

Mr. Prayag stated that the family members had discussed the possibility of eye donation but it was decided that since Tendulkar had not expressed such a wish it would be improper to do so. Tendulkar who was in Pune, since he was last discharged from hospital had refused to go back to Mumbai."

According to his wish his last rites were performed at the Vaikanth electric crematorium and prominent theatre and film personalities including Mohan Agashe, Satish Alekar, Haider Ali, Amruta Subhash, Amol Palekar and Atul Pethe, university of Pune vice-chanceller Narendra Jadhav paid last tribute to Tendulkar at the crematorium.

➢ **Condolence Messages on Vijay Tendulkar's DeathPresident Pratibha Patil** said in her condolence message "Vijay Tendulkar was not only an acknowledged figure in Indian literature but also helped Marathi and all of Indian theatre attain recognition at the international level."

➢ **Prime Minister Manmohan** Singh in a condolence message to Tendulkar's family said, "his strog espousal of women's empowerment and the empowerment of the downtrodden has shaped public consciousness in post independence India."

➤ **Leader of Opposition L K Advani** also paid glowing tributes to Tendulkar. He said the playwright was an outstanding writer who gave Marathi theatre a national and international profile."His place, many of which were translated into Hindi and other Indian Languages, were both creative and carried a strong social message,"

➤ **Maharashtra Chief Minister Vilasrao Deshmukh** also condoled the death of eminent playwright Vijay Tendulkar.In his condolence message, Deshmukh said: "The nation has lost the literary genius and dramatist par excellence. With Tendulkar's death an eventful era has come to an end."

➤ Noted film **director Shyam Benegal** said : "Tendulkar was one of the greatest playwright of Indian theatre in the last 50 years. Tendulkar wrote screenplay of my films "Nishant" and "Manthan". I respected his creativity and admired him as a human being." "He was a senior professional form our field and his contribution to the Indian theatre was immense," Benegal added.

➤ **Film director Govind Nihlani** said : "Tendulkar brought modernity to Marathi theatre. He pioneered a paradigm shift in the vision of looking at society and reflecting it through theatre and cinema."

➢ **Bollywood superstar Mr. Amitabh Bachchan** said : " Vijay Tendulkar was a strong and fearless writer and a great mind. I am deeply saddened to hear the news of his passing away." Amitabh was full of admiration for the man who re-wrote many rules of stage writing. "In today's world it is difficult and though to take a committed stand and pursue it. Vijay Tendulkarji did. And that was his strength. At times this stand is the solitary voice of reason often misunderstood but seldom wrong."

➢ **Amol Palekar said**: "His death is a loss to theatre and literature. wonder whether this losss will ever be recovered. I am glad I could do my share of archiving his entire body of work for the younger generation when my wife Sandhya Gokhale and I organized a Ten Festival in 2006 which went on for a week.

List of Vijay Tendulkar's Works :
One Act :

      Thief Police

      Ratra Ani Itar Ekankika (1957)

      Chitragupta, Aho Chitragupta (1958)

      Ajgar Ani Gandharv (1966)

Bhekad Ani Itar Ekankika (1969)

Ekekacha

Andher Nagari

Collection of Stories :

Kaachpatre (1957)

Dwandwa (1961)

Gane (1966)

Phulpakharu (1970)

Essays :

Kovil Unhe (1971)

Rat Rani (1971)

Phuge Savanache (1974)

Ram Prakar (1994)

Children's Plays :

Ithe Bale Miltat (1960)

Patlachya Poriche Lageen (1965)

Chimna Bandhto Bangla (1966)

Chambhar Chauksiche Natak (1970)

Novels :

Kadambari

Katha Eka Vyathechi : Henry James

Nave Ghar : Nave Ayushya : Grace Jordan

Prempatre : Henry James

Aage Barho : G L Letham (1958)

Gele Te Divas (1958)

Devanchi Manse

Amhu Harnhar Nahi: L E Wilder

Ranphul : S L Arora (1963)

Chityachya Magawar : W W Tiberg

Clarke (1957)

Humour :

Karbhareen : Doroothy Von Doren

Biography :

Dayechi Devta : H D Wiloston

To Aamchayasathi Ladhla (Roosevelt) : K O Pear

Film Script (Marathi)	Film Script (Hindi)
Samana	Nishant
Sinhasan	Manthan
Umbartha	Akrosh
Akriet	Ardha Satya
22 June 1897	Aaghat

Play	Original Title	Original Author	Original Language	Institution	Director	First Show	Pub.	Yrs.
Adhe Adhure	Adhe Adhure	Mohan Rakesh	Hindi	Theatre Unit	Satyadev Dube	11th Jan. 1970	Popular	1971
Lincolon Che Akherche Divas	Last Days of Lincolon	Mark Doran	English	-	-	-	Majestic	1964
Lobh Nasava hi Vinanti	Hasty Heart	John Patrick	English	Rangayan	Arvind Deshpande	-	Parchure	-
Tughaluq	Tughaluq	Girish Karnad	Kannda	Avishkar	Arvind Deshpande	17th Aug. 1971	Niklanth	1971
Vasarach Akra	A street Car Named Desire	Tenesse Williams	English	-	-	-	Popular	1966

Dramatic Works

Title	Institute	Director	First Show	Publication
Ghrihasth (The House Holder)	Mumbai marathi Sahitya Sangha, Drama Wing	Damu Kenkare	1955 Exact date not known	-
Sjro,amt (The rich)	Bharatiya vidya bhavan kala kendra	Vijaya Mehta	12th Dec. 1955	1955
Manus navache Bet (An Island Called man)	Lalit kala Kendra	Damu kenkare	28th Oct. 1956	1956
Madhalya Bhinti (Middle Walls)	Best Art Section	Nandkumar Rawate	4th Nov. 1958	1958
Chimanicha Ghar Hota menacha (The Wax House of the Sparrow	Rangmancha	Vijaya Mehta	27th Dec. 1959	1960
Mi Jinkalo (I Won, I lost)	Rangayan	Vijaya Mehta	20th Oct. 1963	1963
Kavlyanchi Shala (School for Crows)	Rangayan	Vijaya Mehta	5th Dec. 1963	1964
Sarga Sari (Drizzle O Drizzle)	Mumbai Marathi Sahitya Sangh, Drama wing	Arvind Deshpande	18th May 1964	1964
Ek Hatti Mulagi (An obstinate Girl)	Kala Vaibhav	Almram Bhende	21th Nov. 1966	1968

Shatata Court Chalu Ahe (Silence! The Court is in Session)	Rangayan	Arivind Deshpande	28th Dec. 1967	1968
Jhala Anant Hanumant	-	Arvind Deshpande	-	1968
Dambdwipacha Mukbala (An Encounter in Umbugland)	Rangayan	Arvind Deshpande	10th Dec. 1969	1974
Gidhade (The Vulture)	Theatre Unit	Shriram lagu	29th May 1970	1971
Ashi Pakhare Yeti (So Come Birds)	Progressive Dramatic Association, Pune	Jabbar Patel	26th Nov. 1970	1970
Sakharam Binder	Welcome theatres	Kamalar Sarang	10th mar. 1972	1972
Bhalya kaka	Natya Mandar	Arvind Deshpande	5th April 1972	1974
Gharate Amuche Chan (Nice is our Nest)	Welcome Theatre	kamalakar Sarang	28th Oct. 1972	1973
Ghashiram Kotwal	Progressive Dramatic Association, Pune	Jabbar Patel	16th Dec. 1972	1973
Baby	nateshwar	Kamalakar Sarang	29th Aug. 1976	1975
Bhai Murarrao	Theatre Academy Pune	Mohan gokhale	13th Sept. 1977	1975

29

Pahije Jatiche	-	Arvind Deshpande	-	1976
Mitrachi Goshta (A Friend's Story)	Bhumika	Vinay Aapte	15th Aug. 1981	1982
kamala	Kala Rang	kamalakar Sarang	7th Aug. 1981	1982
Kanyadan	INT	Sadashiv Amarapurkar	12th Feb. 1983	1983
Vithala	INT	Sadashiv Amarapurkar	22nd May 1985	1985
Chiranjeev Saubhagya kanshini	Abhishek	Kamalakar Sarang	14th Dec. 1991	-
Safar	Avishkar	Sulbha Deshpande	6th Jan. 1992	-
Niyatichya bailala Ho (To Hell with the Bull of the Fate)	-	-	-	-

2. KAMALA : AN OVERVIEW

Most of the plays of Tendulkar are performed first and published later. But "Kamala" is such an example that within a short period it was performed in four theatres – Marathi, Hindi, English and Gujarati in Mumbai. In "kamala" Tendulkar deals with current issue and points out the drawbacks of "investigative Journalism". The play is based on real incident of India. In modern India, even today in some interior, rural parts of Bihar and Madhya Pradesh women are sold and this was proved by Ashwin Sarin, an Indian Express 'reporter' who actually bought a girl from a flesh market to expose the brutal exploitation of women that exists in rural India. This story belonged to the wave of Investigative Journalism that broke into the staid, decorum-governed news-rooms of the English Language press and also created the magazine boom of the post emergency years. The facts of Sarin's story, however were only a take off point for Tendulkar.

The play presents a self-seeking journalist, Jaisingh Jadav who treats the woman purchased from the flesh market as an object that can buy him a promotion in his job and a reputation in his professional life. He is one of those modern day individuals with a single-track mind, who pursue their goal unquestioningly. Jadav never stops to think what will happen to Kamala after this exposure. Tendulkar makes a jibe at the modern concept of journalism which stresses the sensationalism. In Ashwin Sarin's report "Kamala" was the centre of interest but Tendulkar, here makes the journalist, Jaisingh Jadav a centre of interest.

Tendulkar here reflects on the modern day culture, a blind flight of the people to become reputed in an instant at the cost of negligence of moral values. Today's world is success-oriented and man has become overambitious. He runs madly after fame, name and money. As people worship them who have fame and name, each field of society has become success-oriented. Gone are the days when Mother Teresa or Gandhiji rendered self-less service to humanity and became famous. Today man wants name without any fruitful service to humanity. Tendulkar tries to present such selfish, success-oriented generation of modern India through the field of journalism.

In the name of truth today a newspaper publishes astonishing facts but actually through such sensational news a journalist tries to be popular. Search for truth is only a mask but within it a journalist seeks selfreputation. The play was written in 1982 but it is more relevant today. The community of journalists presented in "Kamala" reminds the readers or viewers today's news channels and their sensational news. Each news channel tries to bring some sensational report in order to be in the market. They make even a criminal a celebrity by sensational reporting e.g. the sentence of 5 years of jail to bollywood star Salman Khan was aired in sensational manner. The case of Rahul Mahajan is also an example. In the same way underworld don Dawood Ibrahim is also made a celebrity by modern journalism and electronic media. The media today gives undue and excessive importance to such people bringing them to the limelight. If Tendulkar were to write a play on journalism today, he must have exposed the new trend known as "Sting Operation" by which the news channels and reporters try to expose the negative traits of the celebrities. But even "Sting Operation" also suffers from drawback as up to now on no one is investigated or penalized due to sting operation.

Let us examine the thematic concerns and the characterization in the play. Thematic concerns is an imaginary thing abstract idea which can be felt, experienced and understood by the readers and viewers. It is that organ of the literary art without which the creation of the writer loses all its worth and value. What is soul to a body, is theme to a literary work. Soul though invisible, gives life and luster to the body of flesh and blood. The same way, theme offers credit and status to a literary work. As a student of the plays of Vijay Tendulkar, I have tried to examine the thematic concerns in Tendulkar's plays. While viewing his plays from the point of view of thematic concern, one thing can be said in general that he deals with the problems of the present day, issues of the existing situations and drawbacks of the so called dignified society. He deals with the multiplicity and themes in his plays ranging from journalism to the problems of deprived class. Whenever a work of literary art contains several thematic concerns at a time in it the readers or the viewers' point plays a very vital role. In such a case, the realisation of theme differs form person to person. The best example of it is **"Kamala"**. It is a play with several thematic concerns. At the first glance, degradation of woman in free India seems to be the theme of this play but the intense reading brings to the surface some more interpretations and meanings. The result is that one viewer may consider the state of woman in the post independent era as the main focus of the play while another viewer may consider instant journalism as the main focus of the play. So theme is not only what the artist wants to convey in a work of art but also what the viewer or a readers considers or what emerges into his mind after watching a work of art.

Vijay Tendulkar's **Kamala** demands and deserves a special applause from every respect and particularly from the thematic point of view. The play is an ideal proof of Tendulkar's dramatic art in a sense that there is a nice blending and at the same time the balance of all thematic points in it. Point counter point, all the thematic issues and concerns are juxtaposed and compared. For example Sarita against Kamala, journalism of Kakasaheb against that of Jaisingh and finally Jaisingh as a journalist against Jaisingh as a man.

Mr. N.S. Dharan writes in **"The tongue-in-cheek" in silence and Kamala".**

"In Kamala, too, Tendulkar makes use of satire in order to scoff not only at the hypocrisy of the urban upper middle class but also at the rampant corruption of the politicians, the cut-throat competition among the journalists and the tenuous relationship that exists between a husband and his wife. Satire, thus, operates at two levels in the play, namely, in the relation of a typical Indian middle class milieux, and also in the social institutions of 'politics', 'marriage' and 'journalism', Kakasaheb is Tendulkar's spokesman in his jibes directed at politicians and journalists. Both Sarita and Kakasaheb become in the playwright's hands, instruments for satirizing the institution of 'marriage'. The satire in 'Kamala' is even more pronounced than that in silence."

(1) Progress oriented modern man,

(2) Condition of woman in Independent India,

(3) Instant journalism

are the main thematic concerns in the play which also present the nature of the characters. Kamla by Vijay Tendulkar is a naturalistic play. It focuses on the changed role of women in society. It was inspired by a real life incident - the Indian Express exposure by Ashwin Sarin, who actually bought a girl from a rural flesh market and presented her at a press conference. But using this incident as a launching pad, Tendulkar raises certain cardinal questions regarding the value system of a modern success-oriented generation who are ready to sacrifice human value in the name of humanity itself. The playwright exposes the innate self-deception of this standpoint. It is the story of an unfortunate woman sold away in the flesh market and a so-called happy housewife married to a daring journalist, both having a revelation of finding themselves on the common platform of sexual slavery in this male-dominated world.

3. PROGRESS ORIENTED MODERN MAN

Jaisingh Jadhav is a well-known young journalist associated with an English daily published by an unscrupulous press baron Sheth Singhania. Sarita is his wife. She is well educated and hails from a village called Phaltan. They live in a small bungalow in a fashionable locality around New Delhi in the neighbourhood of Neeti Bagh. Though highly educated, Sarita lets herself be reduced to the status of a slavish docile wife. He appears at first on the stage dead tired due to journey but seems very excited about the fruit of his successful journey and this is evident when he rings up to his friend and says-

"Hello Jaspalji main Jaisingh bol reyae. I've just come back. Mission accomplished! Yes, brought her with me......what time have you fixed the press conference? That's wonderful. Is everything else ready? Excellent ! they can still prosecute me? Let them proceed. That'll make a nice front page item. Even more publicity."

This very speech of Jaisingh reflects his lust for fame, which is the ruling motto of present day culture. By exposing the tribal woman in the press, he desires only publicity. He does not have any sympathy for the woman Kamala. She is just only a tool for his success as a journalist so when Kamala proposes to do little work, he comments –

"These downtrodden people are happy at the slightest excuse. Toil and labour take getting used to, Luxury doesn't".

Thus, he laughs at the mentality of the downtrodden who like to work and to do labour. In the modern culture, people do not put trust on others and likewise Jaisingh informs about his mission to his wife Sarita only that he has brought Kamala from the Luhardaga Bazaar in Bihar for 250 rupees. In order to prove that such auction of women is prevailing in India today. He supports his mission by blaming the police and the government. He feels proud that he is the first journalist who reached there and brings it to the notice of the people. Through the exposure of Kamala in the press conference Jaisingh wants to prove the degradation of moral values in modern world but he does not know that he himself has become a part of such a degrading society as he says,

"There is a way of doing these things. You have to build them up that way. What's so unusual about Luhardaga flesh market? Women are sold in many places like that, all over the country. How do you think all the red- light districts could operate without that? That's not the point. The point is how we project Luhardaga – the technique of it. The art lies in presenting the case

– not in the case itself! Keep watching. See how we'll blast out this shameful affair. There'll be high drama at today's press conference. It'll create an uproar."

So, he wants his own publicity as a journalist. He is a man of double standards. By exposing Kamala at the press conference he wants to prove himself as a saviour of women but inwardly he wants his own recognition as a journalist so he prevents Sarita who wants to lend a Sari to Kamala as she is in tattered clothes. He wants to present her as she is and it shows the deadened sensibility of modern man. Thus Jaisingh Jadav, appears as a self-seeking journalist who treats the woman he has purchased from the flesh market as an object that can buy him a promotion in his job and a reputation in his professional life. He is one of those modernday individuals with a single-track mind who pursue their goal unquestioningly. Jadav never stops to think what will happen to Kamala after this expose. Through Kamala's exposure he wants to present the exploited status of women but if we evaluate his own personal life he also appears as traditional husband who dominates his wife at home.

Sarita, Jadav's wife, is also an object in Jadav's life — an object that provides physical enjoyment, social companionship and domestic comfort. He talks about equality, freedom of woman but at home he does not allow these. He likes that his wife should perform the role of ideal Indian house wife, obedient wife. She performs the role of ideal wife as she notes down all his phone calls if he is not present, prepares delicious meals for him. She is so docile that Jaisingh's friend Jain used to call her **"Lovely bonded Labourer"** and this very phrase indicates a lot about Jaisingh's treatment of his wife. Sarita is not aware about her own exploitation but the entry of Kamala in the house awakens her conscience. When Kakasaheb says that Kamala is just a pawn in Jaisingh game of chess, Sarita says :

"Not just Kamala, Kakasaheb. Not just Kamala, Kakasaheb, Me too............me too"

So Tendulkar tries to present the contradiction in Jaisingh's personality. Before the society he projects himself as a man who holds liberalism for women, a person who advocates the philosophy of equality and freedom for women but at home he performs the role of the master who suppresses his own wife, treats her as a slave, not better than Kamala as Sarita says – "Kamala, showed me everything....... I saw that the man I thought my partner was the master of a slave."

In his blind flight towards success Jainsingh fails as a husband also. Mr. **N.S. Dharan** writes in **"The tongue-in-cheek in silence and Kamala".** "In fact Jadav, the successful journalist turns out to be cruel not only towards Kamala but also towards his own wife Sarita. Kamala to him, is only an object that helps him win instant fame as a journalist......"

Sarita, to him, is, again, an object to be paraded as a wife at parties, to enhance his status as a successful journalist. In essence, he is the typical Indian husband, who has no time to spare for his wife assuring her of his affection for her. In short, it is the husband-wife relationship, that has come under increasing threat in metropolitan cities like Bombay which has been the butt of satire in Kamala.

Both Kakasaheb and Jain refer to Jadhav as an irresponsible husband whose craze for publicity overwhelms him so much that he totally ignores her very existence. In one instance, Kakasaheb, referring to Jadhav's thoughtlessness, tells Sarita. "This is something that concerns the whole life of one of our girls-your life. We didn't give you to him, to take you back as a window". (KL7). In response, sarita tells him. "But you did give me away didn't you." Then that's that" (KL7)

To Jain, Sarita is simply Jadhav's "lovely bonded labourer"(KL 17) There are repeated hints in the play to show that the husband wife relationship between Jadhav and Sarita has, in fact, deteriorated to a disgraceful master- salve relationship.

On one occasion, Jadhav wants Sarita to send Kamala to him at once: Jaisingh : (Looking at his watch) Sarita ! Hey, Sarita !

(Enter Sarita), What"s she doing?.

Sarita   : She's asleep. She isn't feeling well.

Jaisingh   : Wake her up.

Sarita   : She's only just gone off to sleep.

Jaisingh   : Never mind. Wake her up and send her

here. I want to talk to her. (KL 18-19)

All Jadhav's bravado vanishes into thin air when in the end, he is confronted by a defiant Sarita. In the following conversation, Tendulkar satirizes the utter impotence of the 'macho' males who find themselves suddenly emasculated when confronted by enlightened women.

Jaisingh : Come Upstairs

Sarita : [Emphatically, without even realizing it] No.

Jaisingh : I'll have my dinner afterwards. We'll both eat together.

Sarita : [without losing her self-control.] Uh-hunh, let me go. I've got work to do.

Jaisingh : [Trying to embrace her]. Work later. Come upstairs now.

Sarita : [Throwing him aside with a single shove]. Move aside. What are you doing?

Jaisingh : [Hurt], what's the matter? What didi I do? Why are you making a face like that? Why did you push me away? You've never done that before.

(KL-32)

The following is another episode that throws valuable light on Sarita's recalcitrance:

Sarita : [With greater determination]. Kamala is not going to come with you.

Jaisingh : That's enough of you jokes. Chalo kamala. [To Sarita] Bring her bundle from inside.

Sarita : Kamala is not going with you. She's going to stay here. (KL 41)

The 'Press Conference' that Sarita intends to hold, though in all probability she may not, is aimed at exposing the double standards practiced by chauvinistic males like Jadhav. No spectator of the play will miss the satire in Sarita's words in the following episode. On learning of sarita's plans for the 'Press Conference' KaKasaheb is, at once, startled and amused :

Kakasaheb   : Anyone would think Jaisingh is a slave driver.

Sarita   : Not just anyone, I do.

Kakasaheb   : what on earth happened between you two?

Sarita   : Marriage. (KL 46)

For instance, Kakasaheb observes once: "Our houseboy became the Defence Minsiter,.... He's got one foot in Delhi and the other in Karad. And finally, he's neither one thing nor the other" (KL 5). Towards the close, Jadhav's dismissal results from hi proprietor, Sheth Singhania's questionable association with some political bigwigs of Delhi. Thus, in a sense, we may justifiably call Kamala a political satire too.

Thus, both Silence and Kamala are powerful satires on modern society.

4. CONDITION OF WOMEN IN INDEPENDENT INDIA

The play Kamala does not merely present a satirical commentary on investigative journalism but it also presents the burning issue of modern India – the condition of women in free India. Some critics believe that Tendulkar never tries to reform the society through his drama, but in this play he performs the role of reformer by presenting the exploitation of Kamala and Sarita and the revolt of Sarita.

Though we are living in the 21st century, the condition and status of women remain secondary. She is considered still a weaker sex and is exploited by the male society whether she is educated or illiterate. The male-dominated society never gives her chance to voice her feelings in the house. Her role remains within the house as an ideal house wife to cook, to rear the children and to be obedient to her husband. She is still living in a cage-like situation at home and these very facts of women community are explored by Tendulkar in this play.

Arundhati Banerjee writes,

"From the formal point of view, Kamala has nothing new to contribute to Marathi theatre. But then, Tendulkar has always claimed that it is the content of his work that determines the form. And it is difficult to think of any alternative structure into which the central theme of Kamala could be cast. **But the evaluation of the role of an Indian woman within the institution called** marriage, considered to be the holiest of the holy in our society, definitely provides a completely novel point of view showing that women are still mere slaves to their male owners in Indian society in the latter half of the twentieth century. One should take note here that all three female characters in Kamala are in some way or the other subjected by the dominant male character Jaisingh Jadav, who occupies the center of the plot.

Once again, as in "Shantata.. and Gidhade, Tendulkar explores the position of women in contemporary Indian society. Through Jadav's wife, Sarita who is in her own way as exploited as Kamala, Tendulkar exposes the chauvinism intrinsic in modern Indian male who believes himself to be liberal-minded. Like Kamala, Sarita is also an object in Jadav's life, an object that provides physical enjoyment, social companionship and domestic comfort. Kamala's entry into the household reveals to Sarita the selfish hypocrisy of her husband and the insignificance of her own existence. Yet, like most of Tendulkar's sympathetic women characters, she does not have the spirit to rebel against her present condition. Instead, she extends emotional support to Jadav when at the close of the play he is treacherously deprived of his job. But the dramatist also suggests that Sarita cannot unlearn what she has come to realize and at the end of the play there is a faint hope of attaining independence in the future. Kamala and Sarita are both built of the same material as Leela Benare in Shantata, Rama in Gidhade and Laxmi in Sakharam."

Shanta Gokhale a senior theatre critic, historian, playwright and director, writes in National School of Drama's Journal, May 2000, about women character in Tendulkar plays –

"In some of his most significant plays, Tendulkar presents women in pairs. They are quite different from each other in behavioural traits, class and characters. But underneath these superficial differences lie lives that resemble each other in the ultimate truth of being commanded by men, for their pleasure and under their laws. In Kamala the educated, self assured, Sarita realizes, because of an innocent question asked by a scared, illiterate village woman Kamala –

"How much did the owner pay for you?" how close their respective positions in society are underneath the surface differences of class. This is the first meeting of the two women. Sarita is the wife of the flamboyant investigative journalist Jaisingh Jadav. Tendulkar wants to explore this question – was an auction of illiterate, rural women so very different from the marriage transactions of educated urban women?"

Sarita is a Nora who has stopped short of the final breaking out. She does not make a dramatic exit at the end of the play, however, she has understood her situation as surely as Nora ford. It is the illiterate Kamala, one step ahead of her in understanding what the man-woman relationship is all about, who teaches her to see where she stands."

The account of Kamala's exposure in the press conference shocks her and she reacts –

"So while they were asking her those terrible questions and making fun of her – you just sat and watched, did you?"

For the first time at night she shows her unwillingness in satisfying the physical desires of her husband. On that very night her conscience is awakened by her conversation with Kamala. Let us see –

Kamala – How much did he buy you for?

Sarita   – what?

2Kamala   – I said, how much did he buy you for?

Sarita   – (Recovering) Me? Look here Kamala (Changes
                her mind) For Seven hundred.

Kamala – My God! Seven hundred.

Sarita   – why? Was it too little?

Kamala – (Pauses) It was an expensive bargain, memsahib.

                If you pay seven hundred and there are no children.

Kamala – Memsahib, if you won't misunderstand, I'll tell

47

you. The master bought you, he bought me, too. He spent a lot of money on the two of us. Didn't he? It isn't easy to earn money. A man has to labour like an ox to do it. So memsahib both of us must stay here together like sisters. We'll keep the master happy. We'll make him prosperous. The master will have children. I'll do the hard work, and I'll bring forth the children. I'll bring them up. You are educated woman. You keep the accounts and run the house. Put on lovely clothes and make merry with the master. Go out with him on holidays and feast- days."

Through this conversation between Sarita and Kamala Tendulkar has excellently expressed the condition of women in free India. A role of wife is looking after the family and to bring forth the children. If it is not accomplished, it is a bad bargain. Not only Kamala is purchased from illegal auction at Lahurdaga but Sarita is also purchased legally through marriage transactions. The institution called marriage has given the authority to Jaisingh to dominate Sarita. So when Sarita reacts against sending kamala to orphanage Jaisingh reminds her –

"It's I who takes decisions in this house, and no one else. Do you understand?"

Kakasaheb realises Jaisingh's selfish motive and says that Kamala is just a pawn in his game of chess and Sarita Says –

"Not just Kamala, Kakasaheb, Not just kamala, 'Kakasaheb, Me too…….. me too."

Once Sarita sees herself in the light of a slave, the sole purpose of whose life is to please the master, everything falls into place. She denies to go with Jaisingh in the party which is the first sign of her revolt. Her conversation with Kakasaheb truly reveals that she is awakened against the dominance and hypocrisy of her husband. She too feels that she is purchased like Kamala and that too legally and she says she will call the press conference in order to expose her husband. She says –

"I am going to present a man who in the 1982 still keep a slave right here in Delhi. Jaisingh Jadav. I am going to say : this man's a great advocate of freedom. And he brings home a slave and exploits her. He doesn't consider a slave a human being – just a useful object. One you can use and throw away. He gets people to call him a sworn enemy of tyranny. But he tyrannizes his own slave as much as he likes, and doesn't think anything of it – nothing at all. Listen to the story of how he bought the slave Kamala and made use of her. The other slave he got free – not just free – the slave's father shelled out the money – a big sum. Ask him what he did with it."

Mr. N.S.Dharan writes in **"Gyno-centrism in Silence! and kamala".** "We see both Benare in Silence! and Sarita in Kamala playing roles which anger, mystify and bemuse their male counterparts. They emerge as capable modern women who challenge the male chauvinists in society. In fact, the two plays

Silence! and Kamala are Tendulkar's attempts at delineating women who, inspite of their supposed inferior status in Indian society, rebel against all odds and command our admiration.

The principal action in both the plays revolves around women protagonists. Benare in Silence! and Sarita in Kamala stand for the central consciousness in the respective works of art, beyond any shade of doubt, and hence, the plays can be rightly called women centered. Through them Tendulkar projects a point of view that is peculiarly feminine – tending to be even feministic – as the entire denouement in both the plays in question bears it out. In these women-centered works feministic ideology, which pits women in direct encounter with Chauvinistic male oppressors, finds its full and free expression. In characterization too, Tendulkar has deliberately given his women characters a greater variety and depth – and thus a definite edge, over to their male counterparts. Benare's emotional outburst at the end of Silence! and Sarita's confident and assertive utterances towards the close of Kamala show that both the plays are beyond question, gyno-centric."

So, through her experiences in married life she comes to know that she is treated in the house only as a useful object. The entry and the condition of Kamala awakens her she says –

"I was asleep. I was unconscious even when I was awake. Kamala woke me up. With a shock. Kamala showed me everything. Because of her, I suddenly saw things clearly. I saw that the man I thought my partner was the master of a slave. I have no rights at all in this house. Because I am a slave. Slaves don't have rights, do they, Kakasaheb? They must only slave away. Dance to their master's whim. Laugh, when he says, laugh. Cry, when he says cry. When he says pick up the phone, they must pick it up. When he says, come to a party, they must go when he says, lie on the bed – they."

This dialogue truly shows Sarita's slave like treatment towards Sarita in the house. She cannot prevent her husband when he sends Kamala to orphanage. Her likes, dislikes and opinions are never taken into consideration by Jaisingh. Being woman she is considered weaker and so she asks –

Why can't men limp behind? Why aren't women ever the masters? Why can't a woman at least ask to live her life the same way as a man? Why must only a man have right to be a man? Does he have one extra sense? A woman can do everything a man can."

Catherin Thankamma writes in "Women that patriarchy created : The plays of Vijay Tendulkar, Mahesh Dattani and Mahaseweta Devi"

"In Kamala Jaisingh's indifference to Kamala's feeling is only slightly more pronounced than his feeling towards his wife Sarita. If he expects Kamala to appear at the press conference in her soiled and torn clothes to suit his sense of the dramatic, he expects Sarita to submit to his desire for sex whether she wants it or not. While Sakharam Binder beats up Champa when she refuses to have sex with him, the educated and socially committed Jaisingh calls Sarita "bitch". Yet Sarita meekly accepts her subordinate position in the house, willingly following every instruction to the last detail. It is only when she sees Jaisingh's commodification of Kamala that she realizes that there is an essential difference between Kamala and herself, but whatever resentment or desire for an alternate future that she feels gets watered down to two gestures – giving an identical Sari to kamala and expressing the pious hope that someday things might change. It is interesting that the uncle Kakasaheb who first sympathizes with Sarita and is critical of Jaisingh ends up telling her that men are like that and that her place is beside her husband. In a subversive way he is ensuring the continuance of the status quo, and Sarita agrees. One wonders whether it is an act of self-sacrifice or a mere product of social conditioning. It is most likely a blend of the two......."

She is awakened but being an Indian woman she remains a source of support to Jaisingh when he is sacked from the job. Her conscience does not allow her to leave her husband helpless when he needs a moral support of his life partner. She fulfills her duty as an ideal wife and tries to forget her own slavelike situation in the house. So Shanta Gokhale writes –

"Like Nora she too might have decided to leave her husband at that point. However Helmer has just escaped public dishonour by the skin of his teeth and is now so full of himself that he graciously offers to "forgive" Nora for her crimes, thus confirming all her doubts about his love for her. His sheer self-centeredness and hypocrisy give her the last impetus to leave. Jadav on the other hand, is betrayed by his editor after all the credit he brought to the newspaper with his press conference. He is to be sacked for stepping on powerful toes. Sarita defers her own decision about the future in order to give him the moral support he needs. She may have decided to stop being a slave, but not to stop being a compassionate human being."

Vikram Gokhale, who played Jadav in Kamala raised a doubt regarding the role of Kakasaheb. He ask, "where does Kakasaheb stand vis-à-vis her treatment at the hands of husband? Why does the old man who argues against exploitative journalism, not argue equally vehemently against exploitative husbands?" Let us see Kakasaheb's conversation.

Sarita	– why does a successful man not become a better human being? Why does he turn into an owner"?
Kakasaheb	– There's only one answer to your question Sarita. That's the way men are. That's why they are men……. I was no different, let me tell you. Don't go by what I am today. I've harassed your aunt enough. As my right I didn't give a damn what she felt. I kept my eyes on the road ahead. She allowed herself to be dragged after me.
Sarita	– And that's how you too should be, Sarita. Follow your master dumbly. That's your duty.
Kakasaheb	– It may be painful, but that's the truth. If the world is to run, marriages must work, and if marriage are to work this is the only way."

Gokhale would have liked the uncle to be a flag-waver in the women's cause. But, as we have seen, Tendulkar's case is that all men are exploiters of women, even those who wear the garb of education and liberalism.

Vikram Gokhle On Kamala :

Through the agency of the troupe, Kalarang, we did approximately one hundred and thirty snows of Kamala throughout the length and breadth of Maharashtra and finally in Delhi itself.

While doing these shows I undoubtedly got the satisfaction of doing something innovative. But unfortunately we could not strike a chord with the writer of Kamala...... I had, and still have some serious objections to Tendulkar's treatment of characters in Kamala. May be they are all wrong but they are there. .. . . I had these basic doubts while doing Kamala and these are still there even today (in 1991). I have spoken about them to Tendulkar himself in our discussions but his vague answers did not satisfy me nor do they today. I suppose there may be some deficiency in my own understanding or I may be making some mistake.

If one looks at the conversation between Sarita, Jaysingh's wife, and Kaka Saheb in the second act and also at the ending of Kamala, one does not get any clear picture of what Tendulkar the dramatist says or wants to say...... this question of mine then has remained unanswered even today. I believe Kamala is not only a "good story" and Tendulkar is not a mere story-teller. Sometimes I wonder whether this sensitive dramatist, one of my favourites, was becoming an escapist in the writing of Kamala.

Whatever be the case I would like to say that Tendulkar the man has unfortunately got the better of Tendulkar the dramatist in this play. I would have loved to get answers to my questions form the dramatist himself. Inspite of my repeated requests Tendulkar did not attend the rehearsals even once. Let alone an entire show Tendulkar has not seen even a small part of any show, even from the wings although he heard the news of our closing down the shows.

He might have his own reasons but I have never understood the following things. I am not sure whether for Tendulkar a woman in a maledominated society, no matter where she is, no matter of what religion or caste, no matter educated or uneducated is necessarily a Kamala or whether Kamala is a particular tendency. I do not know whether she represents masochist tendency or whether she is a parody of some of the orthodox Indian notions of the wife's duties. Similarly I am not sure whether Jaysingh is supposed to be a victim of the opposite perversity sadism or of something else.

As I see it there are three reasons that give rise to these questions. (1) The entire character of Jaysingh Jadhav and his ideology. (2) the character of Kaka Saheb, and the gap between his words and deeds. (3) the gap between the thoughts and ideas centering round Sarita Jadhav, and the ending of the play.

In a public discussion on the play some ten years ago I had voiced my feelings about Sarita Jadhav. I had said that she is a frigntening representative of the orthodox Indian wives. If one looks at the ending of Kamala, one wonders whether Tendulkar wants to suggest that Sarita, because she represents Indian wife, is a masochist, and if so does she remain so because she has no other alternative. Further, even as the champion of idealistic journalism Kaka Saheb comments on his nephew Jaysingh wallowing in the mud of yellow journalism, and on his rude behaviour with his wife, he also speaks about his own married life and tells Sarita a thing or two from his own experience of life. Now in doing this it is not clear whether Kaka Saheb cynically mocks at Sarita's suffering by telling her that she has no alternative or whether he is trying to gloss over his own male chauvinism. It is not certain whether he really opposes Jaysingh or not. If he does, to what extent? There are many such tormenting questions about Kamala which the play does not answer. At least I have not got the answers either from the play or form the playwright.

The condition of women is best reflected through Kamala's character and her condition. The women in free India still live in degrading situation and Tendulkar presents it by the auction of women in Luhardaga. She is uneducated rustic lady. She readily agrees to come with Jaisingh as poverty compels her to become a part of such an auction. For her this auction is a means of survival. By which she will get home, and children. Being a woman, she needs only a roof which can provide her shelter for lifetime. Since she is purchased, she knows that her duty is to fulfill all the desires and orders of her master. She never thinks like Sarita that she is exploited. On the contrary she suggests how both of them can live under the same house and fulfill the master's wishes. For her every woman is purchased from the market so whomsoever she meets, she asks how much the master paid for her. So she even asks Kamalabai, the maid servant if she is bought or hired. The same question she asks to Sarita how much did he buy for? So for her the destiny of a woman is to be sold only. And she is so much ignorant that she does not feel that she is being exploited. Her conversation with Sarita best reflects her mentality.

Kamala   – My word! What a big house. And so beautiful.

            Even our Roya's palace isn't as beautiful.

Sarita   – Do you like this house, kamala.

Kamala – It's got everything. Just like a dream. Really.

            Where does he sleep?

When she comes to know that her master has no children and he paid 700 rupees for Sarita she innocently utters –

"It was an expensive bargain memsahib. If you pay seven hundred and there are no children...."

She is ready to work hard from morning to evening even in the fields. She feels sorry that her master has spent lot of money on two of them. So now it's their duty to keep him happy. She suggests that she will work in the house and bring forth the children whereas Sarita being educated will keep the accounts and will attend the parties. She has not the least idea that she will be presented in the press conference and she is merely a tool for Jaisingh to get promotion and reputation as a journalist. She is unaware about the ways of city people so she keeps smiling when all such kinds of strange and odd questions are asked to her. She is unwilling to go to an orphanage but Jaisingh persuades her by saying that It's nice place. Her departure from the house is presented by Tendulkar like this – "Kamala goes to the door as if she is being dragged there."

So, Kamala's situation reflects that in interior parts of India women are still suppressed. They are sold as a slave and they too accept it as a means of survival. They never demand a status like wife, who should be an equal partner in the life. Their concept of wife is to bring forth the children and to work and Kamala is ready to perform both these duties if a home is provided to her.

Maya Pandit writes in **"Family in Tendulkar and others."**

"Kamala dealt with the problem of the negligible value of woman as a commodity in the modern world. Both Kamala and Sarita are commodities which can be sold off for cash or kind. Kamala asks Sarita – "How much did the master pay for you?" The innocent question brings out the truth that in a country like India whether it is a tribal woman or an urban educated lady, their fate is basically the same. For kamala, the division of labour is simple she will give birth to children and produce heir for the Master's property and Sarita can go out with him, provide him with intelligent company. Here Tendulkar also seems to be critiquing the concept of companinate marriage which had been popularized by so much of the canonized literature. Kamala also showed how even the state machinery is involved in the heinous crime of trafficking in woman. And even press, the fourth estate colludes with the state as an ideological apparatus of power to maintain status quo of unequal relations in society Jaisingh, Sarita's husband, is a journalist of commitment as he calls himself. But this commitment is less to human values like freedom than to sales and advertisement as Sarita points out. Jaisingh is a pukka representative of the patriarchal ideology of what it means to be a husband. "It is I who takes decisions in this house and no one else" he tells Sarita. His house and his wife are noting but the things to be owned. His expectation that as wife Sarita's duty is to fulfill and satisfy all his demands sounds absolutely like Sakharam. Therefore as Sarita points out, he is like an owner of slaves. Her rage is manifest in her question "When a man becomes great, why does he have to become a great owner and not a great human being?

The answer to that is provided by uncle. –

"Because he is born as a male."

This is exactly what Sarita challenges – "This must be changed," she asserts and dares to dream –

"The day will come when I will cease to be a slave. Then I shall cease to exist as a thing to be used and thrown away. I will do everything but not because someone orders me to do it. No one shall rule over me. That day will definitely come. I will pay any price for that dawn."

So in Kamala Tendulkar tries to present multi thematic concern. Through each character Tendulkar discusses new issue.

Each character has his/her own personality and ideology and his\her action provides new dimension to the play.

5. INVESTIGATIVE JOURNALISM

V/S

GANDHIAN JOURNALISM

Tendulkar's first job was in a printing press. He then moved into journalism, serving as a subeditor on the daily "Navbharat" then as executive editor of the magazine Vasudha and Deepavali, then as subeditor on the daily Maratha. He also worked as assistant editor of the daily Loksatta in 1968. So in his professional experience as a journalist he has observed the lot of journalist, the new trends in journalism and all that he has presented here. In this play he tries to examine the investigative journalism V\s Gandhian journalism. Jaisingh Jadav is an investigative journalist. His concept of newspaper reporting is shown in a critical light with Kakasaheb, a journalist of the old school, providing the true ideals of journalism.

Kakasaheb is a journalist of Gandhian age who fought against the British through his paper. He laments that the real motto of journalism is dead. He says to Sarita.

I'm honoured. Who asks after me now? I'm a back number. – A remnant of times past. A dead journalist – who's just about staying alive! Now it is the day of your husband's type of journalism. The High-speed type! Something catches fire and there he runs! …….. Eye-witness report ! **Being on the spot – that's what is important! Never mind what you write."**

He makes a comment on the new concept of journalism which gives only the detailed account of the incident and does not suggest any remedy. He clearly points out the drawbacks of the new concept of journalism. He says –

My dear, it's not the facts of **an occurrence** that are important. But the topic is. **Discuss** that. **Comment** on it. **Suggest** a way to stop it – suggest why waste our country's time and ours, writing accounts of them? What sort of journalism is it that smacks its lips as it writes blood-thirsty descriptions instead of commentry? It's business isn't news – it is bloodshed!"

"In the very opening scene of Kamala there are numerous satirical hints in which Kakasaheb refers to the "High-speed" journalism practised by Jaisingh Jadav, the husband of Sarita, his niece. He pooh-poohs his craze for "Eye-witness report saying" Being on the spot-that's what's important! Never mind what you write."

When Sarita, in an attempt to defend her husband, tells Kakasaheb "If it's (murder, bloodshed, rape, atrocity, arson) happening shouldn't he observe it? He replies

"Why does he have to? My dear, it's not the facts of an occurrence that are important. But the topic is. Discuss that, comment on it, suggest a way to stop it- suggest that.

Kakasaheb, himself the proprietor of a small vernacular daily, is quick to discern Jadav's real motive behind his reckless and foolhardy news – reporting. Hence, when Jadav says "there's a commitment behind it, there's a social purpose... the common man ....needs to be shocked into at the truth.... We need a force that will raise his consciousness prepare him to struggle for social and political change." Kakasaheb says – "But you are doing all this for the small percentage of the common people who have the good fortune of knowing English. And these fortunate people are going to effect a change in the government of this county. The rest of the population- the majority – poor things are going to carry on in their haze. Because they don't know English.

Formerly the motto of journalism was to bring awareness among the people, to awaken them about the social evils but the modern concept of journalism only outwardly shows the former motto – to bring awareness but inwardly the journalist wants name, fame and money by making the reports sensational. A journalist gets not only fame but also material gain by the sensational news and Kakasaheb points out to Sarita that Jaisingh was living five years ago in small house at Karol Bagh and now he lives in a bunglow in Neeti bagh with servants, car and travels by plane all over the country, stays in five star hotels, along with invitations from foreign embassies. So within five years Jaisingh prospers a lot by his profession.

Jaisingh tries to defend his profession against the allegations of Kakasaheb by saying that there is a commitment behind it. He says – "The common man is living in a kind of unconscious haze today. He needs to be shocked into looking at the truth now and then. We need a force that will raise his consciousness, prepare him to struggle for social and political change."

So according to Jaisingh the common man of India is unconscious about the social and political changes and through such investigative journalism they are making them conscious. But Kakasaheb sarcastically points out the shallowness of new journalism by saying that they are awakening the common man by writing in English! How many average Indians know English that they will read such reports? Kakasaheb becomes angry and reacts –

"This new journalism of yours – if money making is not the object of it – then it's a vandhya – sambhog. In case you don't understand these difficult Marathi words. I'll explain what I mean is – nothing will ever come of it. Arre. Write the people's language first. Speak it. Then try and teach them." The difference between Gandhian journalism and the new journalism is best reflected in the scene of press conference when Kamala is presented. It brings about the shallowness, hypocrisy and vanity of new journalism.

The scene represents self-seeking lot of journalists who in the name of moral values embarrass Kamala at the press conference by asking her odd questions. While asking her questions the journalists forget the concept of gallantry and reverence for women. The press conference is not represented on the stage but Jaisingh and his friend Jain discuss about the questions which were passed to Kamala in the conference. In order to know Kamala's story and flesh market at Luhardaga the following humiliating questions were asked to Kamala at the conference.

- "What are the important social questions in your area?"

- "What are your opinions about the economic exploitation of the tribals?"

- "If there is free sex among you what do you do with the illegitimate children?"

- "How many men have you slept with?"

- "From where Jaisingh Jadav bought you? Tell me the truth. Was it in the bazaar? Or did he came home?"

- "You must have had some free sex with this new Sheth – tell us something about it – how did it compare?"

All these questions simply expose the modern concept of journalism, who in search of fame, forget humanity. In the conference they just torment the ignorant tribal lady and mock at tribal traditions. This tribal woman Kamala becomes only a medium or a tool to decorate their front page. It also shows that a modern man gives respect to only a fashionable woman and it vanishes as he deals with ignorant rustic woman. Kamala, being ignorant only laughs when such humiliating questions are asked.

Kakasaheb cannot tolerate this account of conference and cries out in agony –

"This is your press conference!"

And Jaisingh again tries to defend his profession by saying that they also ask serious questions if the subject is serious. This comment of Jaisingh again shows his vanity as a journalist. For them it was only a "Tamasha" and Jaisingh calls it a "Drama". They mock at Kamala by saying that she is an excellent actress and today she has knocked down even the heroines like Shabana and Smita Patil. After the conference Kamala becomes a useless thing and Jaisingh decides to send her in women's house. He thinks she will live in a better way by getting home, meals and no works for living. Sarita is against sending her at the orphanage. Kakasaheb realizes Jaisingh's selfish motive of self-recognition as journalist by Kamala's exposure at the press and he says –

"Kamala is just a pawn in his game of chess."

Tendulkar also depicts the true nature of the rat-race that goes on in this milieu by introducing Jadav's collegues. Jaisingh, who has brought reputation to his newspaper, becomes victim of his selfish collegues. He is sacked from his job because the proprietor of his newspaper is pressurised to sack Jaisingh as big people are involved in this flesh racket.

6. DRAMATIC TECHNIQUES OF KAMALA

Drama is basically a performing art, which demands enactment on the stage.

Of course, it is equally accepted as literary art. A dramatist has to take into consideration points like stagebility, possibility or creating scene on the stage and effective enactment while writing a play. Dramatic techniques are different from stage techniques. Dramatic technique comes to the rescue of a playwright. While writing a play stage technique is to be employed by director of a drama, and stage manager in co-ordination when the actual enactment or performance on the stage takes place, dramatist employs different dramatic techniques in the writing of their plays as per the demand of the scene and appeal to be made to the spectators. Shakespeare's "Play within play" or Soyinka's "Mime within play" are some of the examples of dramatic techniques. Girish Karnad has also made extensive use of dramatic techniques in his plays like "Hayavadana" and "Nagmandal" In

"Hayavadana", Girish Karnad presents half man and half horse to highlight the idea of imperfection from which man suffers. The same play witnesses the use of mask and interpolation of "Sutradhara" which can be considered dramatic techniques of Karnad. Even in "Nagamandal" the dance of the flames and the conversation among the flames are the same type of devices used by Girish Karnad. Tendulkar's "Kamala" does not witness extensive use of dramatic technique. But a close reading of the play brings to the surface certain techniques employed by Tendulkar.

It seems that Vijay Tendulkar has tried to show his affiliation to the Greek principle of the three unities in the writing of Kamala. The dramatic technique, the unity of time, place and action have been faithfully observed by the playwright.

The Greek principle of the unity of time allows only single revolution of the sun in the life of the protagonist and 'Kamala' observes it. The play begins with the scene of morning and ends with the scene of next morning which fulfills the condition of the presentation of only 24 hours of the life of Jaisingh Jadav.

The same way unity of place has been taken into consideration by Tendulkar. The action of the whole play takes place within the house of Jaisingh Jadav. Neither Luhardaga nor the place of press conference have been presented on the stage. Both these places do not form a part of the actual scene of the play. They have been just referred to and commented upon by Jaisingh during his conversation with Kakasaheb and Mr. Jain. The ugly action of asking improper and immoral question to 'Kamala' at the time of press conference does not form a part of actual scene in the play. The spectators come to know about it only through the conversation among other characters. Indirectly the play fulfills the condition of the unity of action. The observance of the three unities by Tendulkar offers a greater stagebility to the play – the play does not require so many stage devices and techniques because the action of the play takes place within one house.

One more striking device employed by Tendulkar is the absolute absence of the particular scene of the press conference which is the center of curiosity for all readers and spectators. The play creates first a curiosity what would happen at the time of press conference and the climax of that curiosity gets transformed into anti-climax when they realize that the press conference is over. The curiosity of the readers and spectators is satisfied through the exchange of dialogues among rest of the characters. Tendulkar knows the art of creating curiosity in the mind of the spectators to see a particular scene not showing that scene at all and yet how to satisfy his spectators by informing them everything about that scene which is not enacted at all on the stage.

About its dramatic technique **Mr. N.S.Dharan** writes in **"Salient structural Features in Silence! and Kamala"**

"In Kamala a two-act play, we find almost all the structural features that we find in Silence! Except the 'play-within-the-play' motif. It is a more compact play dealing with lesser number of characters and issues. There are in Kamala, brief but highly significant spells of silence, registering the sensitive tragectories of thought processes in the minds of the characters. Added to certain other structural features of Silence!, we have in Kamala the motif of hectic phone calls which contribute to the principal theme of the play. Moreover, there is a deliberate manipulation of lights to indicate the passage of time which we do not find in the former play.

The phone calls in Kamala are significant in that they indicate how busy and well-known Jadhav, the journalist, really is. It is when he is away that the phone rings so regularly that Kakasaheb asks Sarita: "why don't you make Kamalabai sit by the phone?" (KL 4). Some of the calls threaten Jadhav with murder, and one such call happens to be attended to by Kakasaheb, who observes in an anxious tone: "Is it really necessary for Jaisingh to write all these things, under his own name? Can't he write them "From our correspondent?" (KL 7).

The phone calls also serve to indicate how slavish and claustrophobic Sarita has been reduced to, having been married o Jadhav. She is expected to note down each call and if she fails to do so, Jadhav gets furious with her and abuses her. These phone calls also help the playwright to save on several incidents powerfully conveyed through indirect suggestions. For instance, the most significant' Press Conference' at which Jadhav presents Kamala as an irrefutable evidence of flesh-trade is not presented on the stage at all. Jadhav makes arrangements for the "Press Conference" over phone and on his return from the successful

"Press Conference". He is being congratulated by many over phone.

As per the use of lighting in the play, darkness descends on the stage, for instance, at one point in the opening scene. It is used to indicate the passage of time form morning to afternoon. The lights gradually grow dim in the middle of the second Act to indicate that Sarita, sitting alone in the drawing room, is deeply withdrawn into her inner self and hence, shut out form the daylight world outside. Again, it is here in the dimly-lit drawing room that Sarita and Kamala converse with each other.

In fact, it is this free and uninhibited conversation that transforms Sarita from being a docile wife into an assertive and defiant woman, who musters enough energy and resources to confront her husband later in the play, as can be seen from Sarita's alert, interrogative style of questioning of Jadhav. "You're taking her (Kamala) to the orphanage; aren't you? How can it be nicer than here?

Jaisingh   : I'm telling her(Kamala) so that she will feel better.

Sarita   : You're deceiving her !

Jaisingh : It's not so bad there, She will like it.

Sarita   : How do you know ? (KL 41)

There are also in Kamala frequent spells of silence hinting at conflicts between Kakasaheb and Jadhav, and Sarita and Jadhav, indicated by a series of dots. For example, when Kakashaeb warns Jadhav of the threats of murder. " They won't always stop at threats ! One day they'll…(KL 9) Jadhav does nor respond to him at all, but keeps himself busy dialling. This gesture of Jadhav shows how indifferent he is to Kakasaheb's concern for his safety.

There are also short pauses and spells of silence in the private conversation between Sarita and Kamala in Act II. Such pauses indicate Kamala's reluctance to speak out to Sarita, and Sarita's curiosity to know about Kamala's real character as the following conversation bears out :

Sarita : what are you thinking, Kamala ?

Kamala : (Still lost in thought). Nothing

Sarita : You must be thinking of something. Tell me.

Kamala : Uuh – hunh.

Sarita : (Waits a little, and then) Come on, tell me (KL 35)

The dialogue between Sarita and Kamala is of immense dramatic significance, characterized by laconic questions and pregnant utterances.

Kamala : … Where does he (Jadhav) sleep?

Sarita : Who?

Kamala : He – the one who bought me.

Sarita : In the room upstairs.

Kamala : … No little ones?

Sarita : What little ones ?

Kamala : Children

Sarita : We don't have any… (KL 34)

The stage directions in Kamala are as elaborate and abundant as in Silence ! which help the readers get at the root of the tensions in the minds of Jadhav and Sarita. Throughout the play

Jadhav is tense and his tension is reflected in the abruptness of his actions and words. To quote from the play.

Jaisingh : Kamalabai ! Just bring Kamala's clothes – quickly.

(Enter Kamalabai from within with Kamala's bundle)

Sarita : (Rather determinedly) Kamalabai, take them back.

(Jaisingh tenses up, Kamalabai in a fix).

Jaisingh : Give them to me…..(KL 42)

Structurally, both Silence! And Kamala are free from any easily recognizable flaw, and both of them are compact. Never for a moment does the playwright indulge in anything for the sake of sheer theatricality. The plot evolves and unfolds itself rather imperceptibly. There are elements of surprise and suspense in them which make the spectator sit on edge, eagerly looking forward to the next turn of events " Reversals' in both Silence ! and Kamala surprise not only the characters in the play but the readers and spectators as well. The radical change that comes over Benare in Silence! and Sarita in Kamala surprise us. The audience have the satisfaction of having witnessed few rarified moments of pure aesthetic delight and intellectual insight divined by an extremely powerful artist.

7. CONCLUSION

None can deny the fact that literature of every time and space springs from the cultural ethos of that time and space. The natural accordance is always to be found between the literature of a particular time, space and society of that time and space. Literature springs from culture and hence with all its aesthetics it proves to be a social and cultural document of that particular time and space. The bond between literature and culture is an everlasting phenomenon. The basic reason why this tuning is to be found between literature and the cultural ethos is the commitment of the writer. Writer experiences a greater commitment to his time and space and writes with a vision of reality as well as responsibility. His aim is to see and sees the prevailing norms of his culture in a real sense of the term and so he becomes a committed person, a committed writer. His status as a writer would be futile if there is no sense of responsibility or tone of commitment in his works. The first thing that can be concluded on the basis of the present research work on Vijay Tendulkar's plays is that he is a playwright with a conscious sense of commitment. A writer who desires to be aesthetic in his approach of writing, should in no way give himself a consent to connive at the prevailing realities of his time, culture and society. Tendulkar remains faithful not only in observing those realities but also in displaying them through his plays. He is a dramatist with commitment to his time and country. His plays are adorned with aesthetic value but he does not try to escape from his commitment. It can be justified more elaborately on the basis of his plays.

As a playwright he holds a mirror through his works before the society which is very much Indian and the society finds its own reflection in that mirror. Nothing of Society – good and evil, high and low, black and white – remains, unseen or unnoticed to him. His plays present before the spectators both the sides of life of an average Indian.

Tendulkar as a playwright reflects both the sides of Indian life – the bright side as well as the dark one. As Gouri Ramanarayan aptly observes "with his exposure to Marathi theatre form childhood and journalistic background Vijay Tendulkar turned contemporary socio-political situation into explosive drama". He has dwelt on the alienation of the modern individual, satirized contemporary politics, forcefully depicted social and individual tensions, portrayed with finesse the complexities of human character and vigorously exploited man-woman relationship in several of his works. Significantly the themes which have engaged his most frequent attention, have been the plight of woman in a maledominated urban middle class society, and the husband-wife relationship as obtained in metropolitan centers like Bombay and Delhi. Vijay Tendulkar portrays the contemporary society and the predicament of man in it with a special focus on the morbidity in his plays. His plays touch almost every aspect of human life in the modern world and share the disillusionment of the post- modern intellectuals. However, he seems to highlight three major issues: gender, power and violence.

A close study of Vijay Tendulkar's plays reveals that Tendulkar is not a teacher or preacher. He is not one of those dramatists who use their medium in the service of their favourite socio-political ideology. He is not out to propagate any particular philosophy of life. Some critics have pointed out leftist interpretation to the plays like Ghashiram Kotwal, Kamala and Sakharam Binder. It shows that his plays are open to diverse interpretations and cannot be tied down to a single line of thinking. So the question whether Tendulkar writes for life's sake or art's sake is pointless. All that we can say is that he seems to favour socialist humanism but it should also be remembered that his plays do not revolve in the orbit of that ideology either.

It is significant to note most of Tendulkar's plays are gyno-centric. He was essentially dealing with a world, which in the guise of the modern ideal of nuclear family rejected woman's independence as a citizen, enforced traditional Hindu-Brahmin norms of behavior, crushed her attempts of gaining freedom and exercised a rigid control on her sexuality and productivity.

Kamala dealt with the problem of the negligible value of woman as a commodity in the modern world. It is also a satire on yellow journalism, practiced by self seeking journalists like Jaisingh Jadav. He is indifferent to the "human beingness" of Kamala, whom he exhibits at the press conference as an evidence of the existence of rural flesh markets in India. Ironically enough, he is capable of sacrificing human values in the name of humanity itself. Both Kamala and Sarita are commodities which can be sold off for cash or kind. Kamala remains after all a tool – in Bihar a tool to satisfy lust, sex and at Delhi a tool to yellow journalism. The husbandwife relationship that exists between Jadav and Sarita is also typical of the sort existing in several cities like Delhi where executive husbands do not find adequate time for their wives who have to content themselves by being mere "Paradable" social being.

In Silence! Sakharam Binder and the Vultures, Tendulkar deals with the unconventional theme of sex and violence, but a shift in his concerns is evident when he professes emphatically that man is constantly and violently seeking after positions of power and he would work on this "basic theme" hereafter. In fact, he became aware of moral values in the modern political system. His dramatic creation reflects his concern for common man who, caught in the matrix of opportunistic ethics of modern world, feels alienated. **Ghashiram Kotwal** shows how a common man hero, seeking, power, confronts the people who are already in power and undergoes an organic change. Though, it is based on historical legend, is not actually a historical play. Unlike other dramatists Tendulkar finds a parallel running between antiquity and modernity.

The analysis of Vijay Tendulkar's plays show that his commitment remains the same in each of his plays. His plays put forth burning issues of the contemporary society and times without allowing himself to interfere. He presents on the stage characters as free individuals who live according to their inner will and inner landscape that gives the touch of reality to his plays. Nowhere his characters sound as puppets in his hands. They live, love and suffer because of their own way of life. They are round and dynamic in nature, whether they remain for short or long span of time before the audience. Tendulkar believed that the playwright needs to be an actor-writer who plays 'roles' as he writes, and it helped Tendulkar in depicting the characters as he was associated with the theatre. According to him characterization in a play is to a large extent revealed through the dialogue. Therefore the playwright must have a mouldable and not a rigid style of writing. He must change his style with every character and Tendulkar as a playwright followed this.

Each of his characters reveal a new pattern of characterization. Sakharam represents the impotent fury of male masochism. Ramakant and Umakant present vulturine instinct of human beings' avarice, cunningness, lust, ruthlessness. Ghashiram represents lust for Power. Jaisingh Jadav's character is study of success-oriented modern man. Mr. Nath of "Kanyadaan" represents Ganadhian ideology. His women characters truly exemplify Santa Gokhale's remark that they are romanticized, idealized or forced to live by their creator's symbolic purposes. They are first and foremost human beings of flesh and blood who drew their features from the widest range of observed examples. They are allowed to inhabit the entire spectrum for the unbelievably gullible to the clever, from the malleable to the stubborn, from the conservative to the rebellious, from the self-sacrificing to the grasping. Leela Benare, Manik, Champa, Seva, are unconventional heroines, whereas Laxmi, Rama, Kamala, Sarita, Lalita Gauri, Jyoti, Mrs. Kashikar appear as victims in the patriarchal world.

"Theatre is a visual medium as much as it is a medium of words. This visual aspect needs to be used properly not only to create a relief in the barrage of continuously emoted words but also to provide powerful visual insights into the complex content of the play. A play staged in a theater is not a radio play to be heard with closed eyes and enjoyed. The visual element in a stage play, if not used properly can work against the magic of words and harm the play."

A play has a structure. Structure does not mean the plot or the story of the play. It is a framework. It is not visible but is felt." These views of Tendulkar enabled him to remain "experimental" in his plays. Even in commercial drama he made room for himself and had maintained his uniqueness. His plays reveal his art in maintaining economy of words, the ability to express maximum meaning in minimum words. His use of language is marked by an intelligent use of the punctuation marks, blank spaces, full stops and exclamation marks are effectively used by him. The play within the play technique in "Silence! The Court is in session" for the first time in Marathi drama opened up a new height of Drama. In "Kamala" the motif of the hectic phone calls, the device of the fading of lights, suggesting, in an oblique fashion are worth noting.

The success or failure of any work of art depends upon its appeal – whether that appeal proves to be transitory or everlasting. A work of art with an everlasting appeal always remains eternal. It will not be out of the way or excessive exaggeration if the same thing is said about Tendulkar's plays. We do notice even today victims like Kamala, Benare, Sarita, Rama, Lalita Guari in Society. At the same time we notice even today males likes Arun, Sakharam, Ramakant and Umakant, Jaisingh Jadav, Ghashiram etc. as long as such characters are there in our society, the appeal of his plays would remain intact. His plays will never lose the quality of relevance with which they have been written.

BIBLIOGRAPHY

PRIMARY SOURCES

- **Tendulkar, Vijay** – *Collected Plays in Translation,* (Oxford University Press, 2003.)

- **Tendulkar, Vijay** – *Ghashiram Kotwal,* Seagull Books, Calcutta,   2002

SECONDARY SOURCES

- **Abrams M.H.** *"A Glossary of Literary Terms"* Macmillian. 1996

- **Abrams Teera**, *"Folk Theatre in Maharashtrian Social Development programme,"* Educational Theatre Journal 1975

- **Babu M.R.** *Political Deformity, In Indian drama Today,* Prestige - Books – 1990

- **Babu M.S.** *"Spiritual Deformity,"* In Indian Drama Today, Prestige Books – 1990.

- **Babu, Sarat M.** *"Indian Drama Today",* New Delhi, Prestige Books, 1997

- **Banerjee Arundhati**, *Introduction Five plays by Vijay Tendulkar ,* Oxford up, Bombay

- **Bhalla M. M,** *"Folk Theatre and operas",* A Handful of Dreams Kantas Book Depot, 1977, Delhi.

- **Bhasin Kamala & Khan Nighat** Said *"Some questions on Feminism and its relevance in South Asia,"* ISBN New Delhi - 1993.

- **Bhatnagar M.K.** *"Indian writings in English"* Atlantic publishers, New Delhi.

- **Bhatnagar M.K.**, *Feminist English Literature,* Atlantic Publishers New Delhi

- **Bhave Pushpa** *"Vijay Tendulkar : A Study in Contemporary Indian Theatre",* Sangit Natak Akademi, New Delhi – 1989.

- **Bhayani Utpal** – સામાજિક નાટક, એક નૂતન ઉન્મેષ: વિજય તેંડુલકર, NavBharat Sahitya Mandir 1993.

- **Das Bijay Kumar** – *Critical Essay on post-colonial literature,* Atlantic Publishers.- 2001

- **Das Bijay kumar.** *"Comparative Literature,"* Atlantic Publishers, New Delhi.

- **Deshpande G.P** *"Modern Indian Drama,"* An Anthology, Sahitya Akademi, New Delhi 2002

- **Dharan N.S.** *"The plays of Vijay Tendulkar"* Creative Books – New Delhi – 1999

- **Dharan N.S.** *"The Plays of Vijay Tendulkar",* Creative Books, 1999

- **Dhawan R.K.** *"20 years of Indian writing",* IAES, New Delhi 1999.

- **Dodiya J.K. & Surendran K.V.** *"Indian English Drama, Critical Perspectives,"* Sarup & Sons – 2002

- **Gargi, Balwant.** *Theatre in India,* New York: Theatre Arts, 1962.

- **Gayle Greene and Coppelia Kahn**, *"Feminist scholarship and the Social construction of woman,"* Making a Difference : Feminist Literary criticism, London, Methuen – 1985.

- **George, K.M., ed.** *Comparative Indian Literature,* Madras: Macmillan, 1984.

- **Gowda, Anniah.** *Indian Drama,* Mysore: Univ. of Mysore, 1974.

- *વણકર ભી. ન – અનુસંધાન, ગુર્જર એજન્સી, ગાંધીમાર્ગ, અમદાવાદ.*

- *વણકર ભી.ન. – નવોન્મેષ, ભગવતી ઓફસેટ , અમદાવાદ*

- *વણકર ભી. ન. – દલિત સાહિત્ય, પૂનમ ઓફસેટ, ગાંધીનગર*

- **Jyenger, K.R.S.**, *Indian writing in English,* Sterling publishers – 1985. New Delhi

- **Karnad Girish** *"Author's Introduction,"* Three Plays, Oxford University press, Delhi, 1994.

- **Karnad Girish** *"Nag Mandal"* & *"Hayavadana,"* Oup – 1993.

- **Kumar, Geeta** *"Portrayal of Women in Tendulkar's Shintata Court Chalu Ahe,"* New Directions in Indian Drama. New Delhi, Prestige – 1994.

- **M. Sarat Babu** *"Vijay Tendulkar's Ghashiram Kotwal,"* A Reader's Companion, Asia book Club – New Delhi – 2003.

- **Madge V.M.-** *Vijay Tendulkar's Plays: An Anthology of Recent Criticism,* Pencraft International, 2007

- **Mehta Jay** – *Zankhi: Glimpse of Marathi Drama and Literature,* Unique offset

- **Naik M.K.** *"A History of Indian English Literature,"* Sahitya Akademi, New Delhi – 1982

- **Naik M.K. and Mokashi S. Punekar**, *Perspectives on Indian Drama in English,* Oxford UP – 1977, Madras

- **Pandey S. and Freya Barwa** – *New Directions in Indian Drama* Prestige Books.

- **Reddy, Bayapa P.** *Studies in Indian writing English with a Focus on Indian English Drama,* New Delhi: Prestige, 1990.

- **Reddy, Venkata K.** *Critical Studies in Commonwealth Literature,* New Delhi: Prestige, 1994.

- **Sarat Babu M.** – *Vijay Tendulkar's Ghashiram Kotwal,* Asia Book Club, 2003

- **Sharma Vinod Bala** *"Critical Perspectives Ghashiram Kotwal"* Asia book club-2001.

- **Sharma Vinod Bala** *"Critical Perspectives Ghasiram Kotwal",* Asia Book Club, 2001

- **Shiply Joseph J.** *Dictionary of World Literary Terms,* New Delhi: Doaba House, 1993.

- **Srinivas M.N.** , *Social change in Modern India,* Orient Longman – 1972

- **Surendran K.V.** *"Indian Writing : Critical perspectives Sarup & Sons."* New Delhi

- **Taraporewala Freya and Pandey Sudhakar** *"Contemparary Indian Drama,"* New Delhi, Prestige Book - 1990

- **Tendulkar Vijay** *Katha* – 2001

- **Vatsyaya, Kapila.** *Traditional Indian Theatre:* Multiple Streams, New Delhi: National Book trust, 1980.

- **Veena Noble Dass** – *"Studies in Contemporary Indian Drama,"* Prestige – 1990.

ARTICLES FROM NEWSPAPERS

- **Rajadhyaksha Mukta**, Times of India – Monday, January 29, 2007., "Times review / Book Mark., "Vijay Tendulkar answers Some questions."

- **Times News Network** "Times of India" Tuesday, May 20, 2008.

- **The Hindu** 3/10/04., The Hindu - Sunday, September 16, 2001.

WEB SOURCES

http://www.rediff.com/news/2008/may/19vijay.htm (died article)

http://www.imdb.com/name/nm0854919/ (biography)

http://en.wikipedia.org/wiki/Vijay_Tendulkar (biography)

http://www.littleindia.com/news/123/ARTICLE/3138/2008-07-15.html (By:

Shekhar Hattangadi)

http://www.hinduonnet.com/thehindu/mag/2005/11/06/stories/2005110600310500.htm (**A rich

tapestry of women's stories**) Sunday, Nov 06, 2005 on kamala

http://salaamtheatre.org/kamala2004.html

www.urdutech.net/.../2008/05/vijaytendulkar.jpg

chat.indiatimes.com/articleshow/753698.cms

www.sajaforum.org/2008/05/obit-vijay-tend.html

http://news.bbc.co.uk/2/hi/south_asia/7407808.stm (death article)

www.hindu.com/.../stories/2007012002590800.htm (ghasiram) (Saturday, Jan 20, 2007)

http://www.hindu.com/mp/2007/01/20/images/2007012002590801.jpg

http://kpowerinfinity.spaces.live.com/Blog/cns!EEA9A8ECBFC1B50B!309.entry (((kanyadaan performance article) (August 11

Vijay Tendulkar's 'Kanyadaan' - An Unparalleled Performance)

www.indiaclub.com/shop/AuthorSelect.asp?Autho... (kanyadaan poster)

http://geekydood.wordpress.com/2008/04/30/silence-the-court-is-in-session/

http://www.quillandink.netfirms.com/Theatrecian/tcreview060506.htm (silence)

www.alibris.com/.../author/Tendulkar,%20Vijay (image)

http://timesofindia.indiatimes.com/articleshow/23796750.cms (article on ghasiram kotwal's performance) (30 Sep 2002, 2309)

http://picasaweb.google.com/suman.nsd/100MEDIA#5196466031138807074 (ghasiram kotwal)

http://www.mumbaitheatreguide.com/dramas/hindi/sakharam_binder_retold.asp (sakharam binder , performance article and photo)

http://www.sepiamutiny.com/sepia/archives/000636.html (photo sakharam binder)

http://www.iaac.us/Tendulkarfestival/VijayTendulkar.htm (photo with cast of sakharam binder)

http://www.bookrags.com/wiki/Shantata%21_Court_Chalu_Aahe (silence)

http://www.bookrags.com/wiki/Ghashiram_Kotwal

http://www.bookrags.com/wiki/Sakharam_Binder

http://www.bookrags.com/wiki/Vijay_Tendulkar

http://www.indianexpress.com/res/web/pIe/ie/daily/19991020/ile20071.html (article, Wednesday, October 20, 1999)

http://passionforcinema.com/a-conversation-with-sir-vijay-tendulkar/ (conversation with tendulkar)

http://shreevarma.homestead.com/bookreviews1.html

www.ingramcontent.com/pod-product-compliance
Lightning Source LLC
Chambersburg PA
CBHW071058280326
41928CB00050B/2547

* 9 7 8 1 9 2 6 4 8 8 1 8 9 *